Set The Standard

A Guide To Prepare You For a Political Campaign

ISBN: 979-8-234-05541-5 (Paperback)

Front cover image by Lexi Lauwers from Pexels via Canva.com

Cover design by Stepanie Liggio

Published by Liggio Media

This book is designed as a guide and was created based on personal experience and is meant to be a working document to help you build your own campaign or participate effectively in supporting a campaign. This book is not intended to be a full guide to a campaign, and it is written specifically to New York State.

Contents

I want to thank those who inspired me to create this guide.

Gloria Correa Cepin and Sara Roccisano have inspired me to take this to the next level. Knowing each of them in business and in personal life has added to my ambition and success.

Ladies, much thanks to you both.

To the overseer who helped me through my campaign and who put eyes on this with some hints, THANK YOU.

To all my friends, family and colleagues who have always supported me, THANK YOU. Your support has propelled me to move forward.

"The liberties of a people never were, nor ever will be, secure, when the transactions of their rulers may be concealed from them."

- Patrick Henry

Introduction

I have compiled this list of what I found to be necessary in running a campaign as a candidate in the state of New York. You may find that in other states the level of government or some of this information may have to be amended.

I had helpful but minimal guidance in my campaign for a state level district race in 2024. The political parties cannot run the campaign. That is up to you. And this is very much like a small business. I have kept the most basic and necessary parts of the campaign here in this workbook to help guide anyone that wants to take the step and lead our city, state and nation at this critical juncture.

I want to take a moment to say, Thank You. This is not an easy endeavor, this is not a guarantee, this is not going to be fun at times. But civic duty was not created by our founders to be fun. It was meant to play an important role in continuing the work they began 250+ years ago.

Running a campaign, volunteering, and being a candidate is a large commitment. Please, when taking this on, wake up every day with a clear mission, a goal and know that many citizens in your district, city, state may not know the finer details of our government and self-governance. You are becoming a steward toward opening that channel of communication.

The title states that I have compiled the information. I used my notes and various websites that I found helpful. There may be other resources available. Please seek it all out.

Good luck to you.

Best,

Stephanie Liggio

New York State

Federal Level Offices:

US Senate (Statewide Race)

US Representative (District Level Race)

New York State Offices:

Governor (Statewide Race)

Lt. Governor (Statewide Race)

Attorney General (Statewide Race)

New York State Comptroller (Statewide Race)

Judges (Not addressed in this workbook)

New York State Offices, District Level:

New York State Senate

New York State Assembly

Local Offices:

City Council (City/Town)

County Legislature

Other Town or County Level positions including Sheriff and Judges

County and Local Offices include School Board, City Council, Attorney General, Borough President, and other various offices; check your local BOE website for more information.

Helpful Links for New York State

New York State Board of Elections: https://elections.ny.gov/

Independent Voter Project: https://independentvoterproject.org/voter-stats/ny

Helpful Links for New York City

NYC: https://www.vote.nyc/

To find voter registration:

https://vote.nyc/page/am-i-registered

Find your poll site:

https://findmypollsite.vote.nyc/

NYC Districts:

https://vote.nyc/page/nyc-district-maps

Another helpful site to gather information would be

Ballotpedia: https://ballotpedia.org/Main_Page

Google

Preparing & Research

This section will help you prepare the details of the campaign and get the basic information needed to be ready to hit the ground running. The more you know about your district the better you can plan to have an effective efficient campaign.

PRO TIP: Understand the responsibilities AND limitations of the office you wish to attain.

Remember:

- ✓ This is NOT a beauty contest.
- ✓ This is a position of *service* for the district and community.
- ✓ Raise the Bar, Set the Standard.

Fill in this information to start the process.

What office are you considering being a candidate for? ______________________________

Candidate Name (Your Name)

____

Candidate for (Office)

____

District

____

County

____

To understand and create a strategy for your campaign, you will need to gather the following information:

1. District demographics such as

- ➢ the average age ____
- ➢ the median income ____
- ➢ how many registered voters are in your district ___________________________
- ➢ how large is the district ____
- ➢ the number of people registered in the district ___________________________
- ➢ the past three (3) election cycle results for the office you are running for

  Election Year________ Number of Votes____________________________________

  Election Year________ Number of Votes____________________________________

  Election Year________ Number of Votes____________________________________

Also note whether this office runs every two (2) or four (4) or six (6) years.

Understanding voter turnout and the demographic of the district will help the strategy you need to build.

You can gather information from:

- BallotPedia (https://ballotpedia.org/Main_Page) and do a search.
- Google searches.
- Your County Chair for the party you may run under may also have some guidance on this issue for you.
- Every county should have a Board of Elections site. My experience is that the information is there, you just need to know how to find it.

If your district spreads over two (2) or more counties, be sure to have demographic information for each area; you may also choose to do demographic analysis by neighborhood depending on the size of the district and other factors.

2. Who are you building a campaign to run against?

- Incumbent or former office holder

  ____

- Length of time in office

  ____

You can gather information on the incumbent or former seat holder to project:

- the number of votes needed ____
- other pertinent information ____

Hint: This information will properly prepare you for the candidate interview process held by the county leaders. The more you know, the better equipped you are to wow them.

PRO TIP: The Board of Elections is a gatekeeper of information, and you will need to work with your county representative to obtain:

- the voter registration list
- absentee lists
- overseas voter lists
- permanent mail ballot/shut in

These lists will help you formulate a plan and will be discussed in the section Petitions and Door Knocking.

3. More information to gather in your district is types of business and industry. Just as important are the business and industries that your constituents feel should be there but are not. This could help formulate plans to bring in with investment opportunities.

- Senior Centers

Name	Address	Contact	Date to Visit

- Nursing Homes & Assisted Living Communities

Name	Address	Contact	Date to Visit

- Businesses such as bodega, barber shop, supermarket, dry cleaner, dance studio, tutoring center, restaurant, deli, bank, bakery, etc.

Name	Address	Contact	Date to Visit

- Schools

Name	Address	Contact	Date to Visit

- Housing Communities

Name	Address	Contact	Date to Visit

- Churches and other faith and community-based organizations

Name	Address	Contact	Date to Visit

- Libraries (and the schedule to hold meetings and town halls)

Name	Address	Contact	Date to Visit

- Parks and other outdoor areas

Name	Address	Contact	Date to Visit

- Train stations and bus stops

Name	Address	Contact	Date to Visit

- Local community groups

Name	Address	Contact	Date to Visit

- Block associations

Name	Address	Contact	Date to Visit

Take time to drive around the district as a tour to make notes of the size, landscape and take the opportunity to recognize the businesses you have and perhaps what type of industry is not represented (dance schools, karate, tutor center).

Include an image of your district here (you can use google to find the map, check to see it is the most up to date as many states have recently redrawn districts from the census).

PRO TIP: Once you become a candidate, your life is for the world to see. Be sure to put your best YOU forward. Be sure to wear comfortable shoes, dress your best and carry some mints.

Now you can prepare a check list of what tasks you need to do. This sample so that you are keeping on target for having the work done in a timely manner. (A detailed checklist will be posted in the End Notes Chapter 10.)

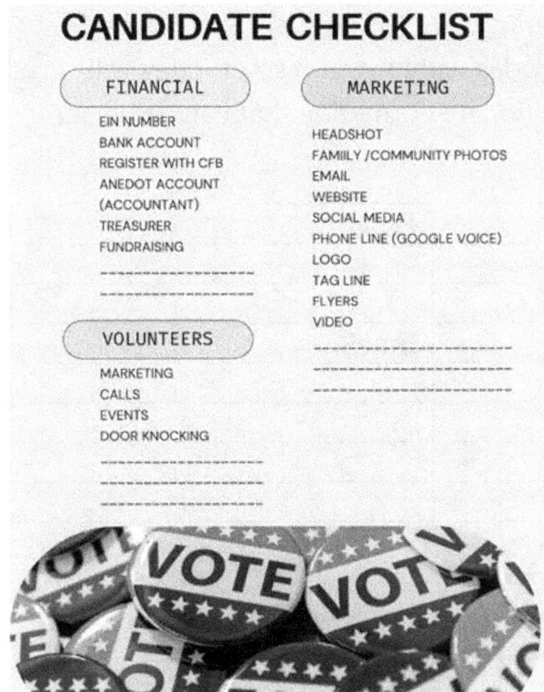

CANDIDATE CHECKLIST

FINANCIAL
- EIN NUMBER
- BANK ACCOUNT
- REGISTER WITH CFB
- ANEDOT ACCOUNT
- (ACCOUNTANT)
- TREASURER
- FUNDRAISING

MARKETING
- HEADSHOT
- FAMILY /COMMUNITY PHOTOS
- EMAIL
- WEBSITE
- SOCIAL MEDIA
- PHONE LINE (GOOGLE VOICE)
- LOGO
- TAG LINE
- FLYERS
- VIDEO

VOLUNTEERS
- MARKETING
- CALLS
- EVENTS
- DOOR KNOCKING

To the left is a sample checklist I created in 2025. You can have a simple checklist like this or compile a more detailed one with deliverable dates and any relevant person on the campaign assisting with the matter.

The checklist should have lists of tasks to complete and you can build it out to include a due date and also if you are assigning a task to a staff member or a volunteer.

Preparation:

- Research
- Conversation with County Chairs
- Conversation with potential staff
- Conversation with potential volunteers

TIMELINE GUIDE: This work should be performed the calendar year prior to running for office to properly prepare for what is to be your campaign.

Also – know who the District Leaders and Committeepersons are (of each party) for your district. Note any overlap that may exist within the zip codes within your district. They will know the registered voters, and they will have some additional information that can be helpful for the campaign.

District Leader	Phone	Email
Committee Person	Phone	Email

In Summary. The more you prepare and are an expert on your district and each neighborhood within the district, the more prepared you are to have an effective campaign.

At this stage, you will need to proceed to the next phase, petitioning, to be on the ballot.

Petition Gathering & Door Knocking

Petition Gathering

This process is a necessary step to actually getting on the ballot and the first opportunity to be on the ground door to door in your district.

PRO TIP: Petitioning is NOT campaigning. Speed and efficiency are paramount.

Petition gathering can take four (4) weeks to get the number of signatures necessary to get the ballot position. Be sure to have an updated voter list that is usually provided by the county political party chair and staff. Also have plenty of volunteers ready to walk some distances and speak to constituents on your behalf. Prepare them to ensure they have the petitions filled out completely and signed by the voters. Each portion of the line has to be filled in, the date, name printed, name signed, address and then the county. Be sure to be well versed in the petition itself and have your volunteers prepared as well.

Also get guidance on how to sign the affidavit at the bottom to insure you are complying with Election Law.

Petition Process Candidate

District Leaders and committee members usually know the registered party members to approach to have signatures obtained for filing. Be sure that all volunteers taking part have been trained to get all the pertinent areas of the form filled in properly to avoid having names removed.

Please also have Voter Registration forms as part of the walking package:

> **PRO TIP:** Know what is needed for the form to be complete so there are no issues when it is turned into the County Board of Elections for input

When the petitions are completed, you will turn them in, this is direction you will need from your District Leader and County Chair. This is when the signatures can be challenged by other parties and can be a grueling couple of weeks. This is why it is imperative to be certain that every line is filled in perfectly and that all voters are confirmed to be registered and within the party line you are petitioning for.

Door Knocking

Door Knocking is necessary to gather support and meet the constituents directly. Be sure that you and your volunteers are aware of the messaging as this is a vital opportunity if there are new people in the area to coalesce support for your campaign forward.

Suggestion: Have a four (4) section notebook to carry with you:

- Log volunteer sign-ups
- A daily journal of places, events attended; people or issues for follow up
- Research that you have gathered as this will continue through the campaign and assist in writing policy and building your platform
- Finances: keep daily logs of receipts, checks (copies), and donations (more under Chapter 3 Financial and Chapter 8 End Notes.

PRO TIP: Be cautious of how much time you dedicate to any one conversation: be cognizant of time and priorities.

PREPARE: Have a script prepared and practiced by all volunteers.

EXTRA: Have a video of you introducing yourself that volunteers can share as they go door to door.

Have a flier handy to leave in case you miss someone at their home. This cannot be your official campaign flyer as you are not acknowledged as the candidate until you receive the official letter from the Board of Elections. This letter will congratulate you and acknowledge you are on the ballot for the primary election and provide that date.

If there is no primary challenger, you will receive a letter after the primary election date stating you are on the ballot for the general election with the date noted.

IDEA: Be sure to gather any names of constituents willing to work with your campaign during this process. This is where the notebook comes in handy to gather names and phone numbers. It is a strong foot forward to engage the community and keep them engaged for the election season.

PRO TIP: If your district has large housing communities, try having a contact person in each community or building to garner support and have people prepared to meet you to gain signatures.

PRO TIP: Be cautious of not becoming short tempered with anyone. Every person you approach may have a different opinion or be over opinionated. Be patient and polite and have a prepared reply so you can easily move on.

GRATITUDE: Good luck to anyone wanting to take this opportunity. We need good voices and experienced people to step into the ring of self-governance.

PRO TIP: You are not allowed to leave flyers in mailboxes without a post mark. (Mailed material only).

Financial & Fundraising Platform

This is one of the most important roles within a campaign. Missing deadlines for financial filings could cause you to pay fines. Not being able to reference the donations into your campaign could also cause some issues.

First, hire your accountant or someone you trust to act as the treasurer.

____

____

Your treasurer needs to obtain the EIN (business identifier number like Social Security Number). The campaign is treated like a separate business and has its own number and gets separate tax reporting post campaign.

____

_____

This will contain your committee's name:

Committee to Elect ____

or

Friends of

____

With this you open a bank account, connect with your bank or another local bank; inquire if there are any monthly fees associated with the account. The bank account cannot be linked to any personal accounts.

It is imperative to keep track of every penny earned and spent. (A suggested format located in Chapter 10 End Notes.)

Next, register with County Financial Board or State Financial Board. Periodically, filings need to be submitted for monies raised. This is performed by the treasurer, but you should have an idea of what happens here as the candidate is ultimately responsible.

You will personally fill in the financial disclosure statement. This is a financial colonoscopy. You are given a chart to use to define the income range to report annual income, asset value for brokerage or investment accounts including the 401k, any deferred compensation you have, Real Estate holdings, and assets of value.

PRO TIPS:

- Keep a daily tracker of donations and expenses as well as receipts for ease in filing. Be sure to have filing dates marked on a shared calendar as well as a physical calendar, so you do not miss these dates.
- You can do this with a notebook log and an excel spreadsheet – See suggested chart at the back of the book.

Create your fundraising platform account by researching the available options: Anedot, WinRed, ActBlue, or other approved platform.

PRO TIP: Be sure the platform is certified by the Board of Elections.

- It is imperative that you investigate your choices and even consult with your prospective treasurer if they have a platform, they are comfortable with or prefer. The platforms give you reports and can also assist with event planning for direct ticket purchases.

Be sure to share your bank account login with your treasurer as well as the fundraising account so they can pull reports necessary for reporting. Do not let anyone else have this login information.

PRO TIP:

New York City Candidates need to register with:

Conflict of Interest Board: COIB; you will receive an email with a liaison that will work with you and assist with your filings.

Build a team

You will need as much support as you can garner. The first level is establishing if you have a budget to hire a campaign manager and if your treasurer is being paid or operating on an in-kind donation. You will need 20 volunteers to do door knocking, calls and other functions. Being prepared with your messaging and your research work on the district will be of great importance for these next steps. Your volunteers will help you reach the outskirts of your district; also help communicate your message.

You can break the district into smaller regions or quadrants and have a paid staff member or trusted volunteer responsible for building out a strategy for those quadrants. Do this based on the district map. If you want to also do this by neighborhood or school district, voting precinct, just know the number of captains or leads you will need.

Volunteers can assist in gathering data, making calls, distributing flyers, setting up events such as: townhalls, meet & greets, listening tours, and fundraisers. Be sure to include everyone in your inner circle that you trust the most.

Volunteers are also needed to walk the district: distribute flyers and gather community support, check in with businesses that are willing to display signage.

Be sure to have a strong presence in housing communities, nursing homes, senior centers, High Schools, any civic groups, any clubs and other gatherings as these areas can be a strong turnout opportunity.

PRO TIP: Do not expect your volunteers or paid staff to work harder than you. Set the standard. Be the Candidate they want to represent the district.

The area District Leaders and Committeemen should know of the volunteers and the trusted votes in the district. Again – know who is assigned for each party in the election districts that are contained in your overall district for the position you are a candidate for.

District Leader	Phone	Email
Committee Person	**Phone**	**Email**

Structure for the campaign:

Candidate

Campaign Manager

Treasurer

Captains

Event Organizer

Liaisons (Business or Housing)

Paid Door Knockers

Volunteers

PRO TIP: Accept assistance and ask for assistance often. Do not try to do it all on your own.

IDEA: Create a lanyard for the staff and volunteers to wear when they are out on your behalf:

Social Media, Website & Marketing

Modern campaigns rely heavily on social media and having an active page gains interest and prominence. You can consider using just social media if you do not have the funds for a full website that can include a monthly hosting fee and any updates you require whether it is daily or weekly.

Keep track of the login and password information for each site and share only with staff/volunteers tasked with accessing these pages. Be cautious to not share the login information with too many people.

PRO TIP: IG gives you a QR code.

Consider having a meeting platform to host meetings and roundtable events online to supplement what you do in person. These can later be clipped to share via social media pages.

Site	Username	Password
Instagram		
Facebook		
X		
Tik Tok		
Locals		
YouTube		
Rumble		
Zoom		
MS Teams		
Google Meet		
Website		
SubStack*		

RESOURCE TIP: Substack, a publishing platform, is a way to blog and post pictures and videos. It could help promote social media sites, prepare you to discuss pertinent topics. Consider starting this prior to the campaign and publish a weekly article and/or video discussing topics pertinent to the campaign. This creates an opportunity to blog an analysis of current budgets and policies.

RESOURCE TIP: Prepare the links to each site to share around, or a QR code to a link tree https://linktr.ee/

STAY HIP: There are also social media managing tools that you can use. This article references a few:

https://technologyadvice.com/blog/marketing/best-social-media-schedulers/

Having a dedicated phone number is great for the campaign. You can set up a second phone line via google voice to accept calls. This saves you the cost of getting a second phone.

- Campaign Phone Number

  ____

Create an email for the campaign. gmail allows for vanity email so can you info@candidate.com in lieu of @gmail.com

- Campaign email

  ____

Marketing

Keep this Checklist for reference:

1. Headshots and other pictures including family, community, if possible also near district icons, memorials etc.
   PRO TIP: Hiring a professional photographer is helpful as they have a natural eye for the imagery.

   IDEA: Note that the background is not the focus and that I am wearing colors that are fun and lively.
2. Logo, keep it clean and simple. As an example, the logo I had (was donated as an in-kind donation and it was basic with clean lines.

3. A tag Line which is a brief line to sum up your campaign. As an example I used "For The People 83". Expressing a sentiment from our founders with the district area number.

4. Press release or a format for statements to be posted on social media as well as holiday messages. (See examples).

5. Create a campaign flyer.
   Prepare 4 x 9 cards that you can have printed to leave behind such as the example I have above.

Use a fact sheet to include background info & biography & policy focus to work through the layout and information to be included. Here is a sample of what I created for my campaign:

6. You will need to regularly create flyers, videos and daily posts with comments on relevant topics

   Canva is a great tool to assist with the marketing efforts; there are other tools to investigate and invest in as well.

Consider the colors and styles that will represent your campaign so that constituents will easily identify the campaign across platforms and around the district.

PRO TIP: You are not allowed to leave flyers in mailboxes without a post mark. (Mailed material only).

PRO TIP: ALL Literature should have the fundraising link, AND contact information.

NOTE: A candidate can be fined for litter if the literature is thrown on the ground (Example: leaving on a windshield and then thrown down.

Messaging PRO TIPS:

- Take three (3) topics that you are comfortable talking about and create policy platforms that you can share out. Be sure the incumbent has a history of discussing this issue to add some meat to the bones for posting on social media pages, blogging or talking points when you meet with constituents and business leaders.
- Provide this information in an easy to pass along format for your volunteers to properly represent your position.
  - LESS IS MORE

IDEA: Come up with ideas for social media that are different than any normal campaign. I created this to share:

FUNDRAISING, EVENTS, CALENDAR

Fundraising

Your network of family, friends, associates and businesses willing to support you will matter most. Plan events that are low cost and fun to gather as many as you can and accommodate different areas of your district.

(Separate guide for event planning to follow)

Some races you will need a considerable amount of money to pay for food truck events, pay for door-to-door flyer to be handed out or to take out ads.

Also, take note of any reporting forms that need to be filled in by the donor and be sure to have a dedicated person at each event ready to manage this vital task.

PRO TIP: Smile, be camera ready, know that people will film you anywhere and everywhere.

Be prepared to host town hall style events in person and via zoom.

Hosting round table events can be effective; keep each focused on the specific issue and invite local people who are considered experts.

Types of fundraising events: Dinners, Online Donations,

Notes:

Events

Set up, check in, overall event coordination. This is very detailed-oriented, and you should have a volunteer or staff member specific to overseeing this as it can take much time for details to be filled.

Calendar of Events (posted to socials and website)

Goal for each event

Any special guests, speakers, experts, other candidates

- Hold roundtable meetings with stakeholders and constituents to discuss these topics and get dialog started. This can be done in-person and via zoom.

Types of events to consider:

Townhall

Meet & Greet

Rally

Food Truck with a Meet the Candidates as a shared event

Seminars – financial literacy, updates on energy, business leader highlight

Plan to attend other events around the county/district:

PRO TIP: Check your local parks schedules for summer concerts and gatherings

PRO TIP: Check the local churches for their community-based events

---

SUPPLEMENTAL – I will go into further planning details in person or in the next guide.

Calendar

Plan out the year(s) on a large calendar that you can share. It is never too early to start attending community events and getting to businesses and community board, PTA meetings.

PRO TIP: Have a daily and weekly plan for volunteers.

Have events listed and planned prior to the year of the election.

Keep track of daily stops into businesses and know where you have support.

Check various apps or programs you are comfortable with to set up a shared calendar with your leads or captains and have a main master paper calendar in your headquarter location.

You may have public and private events, so be sure that your private events are labeled accordingly so that no one leaks any information not necessary to be out in the public.

PRO TIP: Be careful to not over promise yourself to events that are out of district so that you can accommodate being in district as often as you can. Also keep to scheduled appointments as best as you can.

January

Monday	Tuesday	Wednesday	Thursday	Friday	Saturday	Sunday

February

Monday	Tuesday	Wednesday	Thursday	Friday	Saturday	Sunday

March

Monday	Tuesday	Wednesday	Thursday	Friday	Saturday	Sunday

April

Monday	Tuesday	Wednesday	Thursday	Friday	Saturday	Sunday

May

Monday	Tuesday	Wednesday	Thursday	Friday	Saturday	Sunday

June

Monday	Tuesday	Wednesday	Thursday	Friday	Saturday	Sunday

July

Monday	Tuesday	Wednesday	Thursday	Friday	Saturday	Sunday

August

Monday	Tuesday	Wednesday	Thursday	Friday	Saturday	Sunday

September

Monday	Tuesday	Wednesday	Thursday	Friday	Saturday	Sunday

October

Monday	Tuesday	Wednesday	Thursday	Friday	Saturday	Sunday

November

Monday	Tuesday	Wednesday	Thursday	Friday	Saturday	Sunday

December

Monday	Tuesday	Wednesday	Thursday	Friday	Saturday	Sunday

The Debate

Prepare to debate the incumbent on their record and not his/her person. Stay focused on policy. REMEMBER: This is NOT a beauty contest.

You will want to note the key policies they have sponsored, co-sponsored, advocated for:

Bill #	Date	Issue	Committee Pass Date	Floor Pass Date

PRO TIPS:

- You will need to review how many days the incumbent or former office holder was not in person or voted present on any bills. You can also note if they are going along to get along or setting a standard of their own. Get a full picture of their record.
- Take note of the newsletter that the incumbent sends out to you and the constituents; take note of the monies they state are "allocated" for the district, and compare this to the budget passed.
- Take note of community events that the incumbent is promoting.

PRO TIP: Do NOT make this personal. You are a constituent of your opponent and an opponent. Keep this about job performance and the community will rally behind you.

PRO TIP: Be Authentic. It is worth your weight in gold.

SUPPLEMENTAL: There will be more detail and debate prep within person training.

Work Sheets

Here is a suggested format for creating logs for events.

Event Date	Event Lead	Event Location	Venue Contact

Here is a suggested format for logging Financial Receipts (address this with your treasurer)

Date	Amount	Name	Notes	Filled in Form

Suggested format for Volunteer Sign Up (Be sure to assign a lead)

Date	Name	Venue	Email	Volunteer

Suggested format for a Journal entry

Journal Date	Events	Follow Up	Point Person

Suggested format to collect Business information:

Business Name ______________________________

Contact ______________________________

Address ______________________________

Phone ______________________________

Allow Flyer ☐ Allow poster ☐ Willing to host townhall ☐

Business Name ______________________________

Contact ______________________________

Address ______________________________

Phone ______________________________

Allow Flyer ☐ Allow poster ☐ Willing to host townhall ☐

Business Name ______________________________

Contact ______________________________

Address ______________________________

Phone ______________________________

Allow Flyer ☐ Allow poster ☐ Willing to host townhall ☐

Additional Space for Business

Name	Address	Contact	Date to Visit

www.ingramcontent.com/pod-product-compliance
Lightning Source LLC
LaVergne TN
LVHW061258100826
845148LV00008B/1166

* 9 7 9 8 2 3 4 0 5 5 4 1 5 *